VOICES OF ADVENT
LEADER GUIDE

Voices of Advent
The Bible's Insights for a Season of Hope

Voices of Advent
978-1-7910-3631-7
978-1-7910-3632-4 eBook

Voices of Advent: DVD
978-1-7910-3635-5

Voices of Advent: Leader Guide
978-1-7910-3633-1
978-1-7910-3634-8 eBook

MATTHEW L. SKINNER

VOICES
OF ADVENT

THE BIBLE'S INSIGHTS FOR A SEASON OF HOPE

LEADER GUIDE

ABINGDON PRESS | NASHVILLE

Voices of Advent
The Bible's Insights for a Season of Hope
Leader Guide

978-1-7910-3633-1

Cover description for *Voices of Advent: The Bible's Insights for a Season of Hope – Leader Guide* by Matthew L. Skinner. Snow-covered trees beneath a night sky with green aurora appear above a wide gold title band. The words "Leader Guide" are in a gold-framed box at the top. The author's name is in gold at the bottom over a dark blue background with glowing light specks.

MANUFACTURED IN THE UNITED STATES OF AMERICA

CONTENTS

INTRODUCTION

In *Voices of Advent*, Matthew Skinner (Professor of New Testament, Luther Seminary) invites readers to listen attentively to Gospel texts traditionally read during the Advent and Christmas seasons in order to discover what these ancient texts can tell Christians today about expectantly waiting on God. Matt writes, "Advent hope is active hope and not a hope that is content to sit on the sidelines with its arms crossed while watching to see if anything will ever get better." His explorations of these texts demonstrate how they can both spark and sustain our desire "to stay close, to play a part, and to make ourselves available to God."

This Leader Guide has been written to help you lead a group of adults in a study of Matt's book and the Scriptures he discusses. Each of its four session plans corresponds to a chapter in *Voices of Advent:*

- Session 1: The Voice of Jesus—Advent "begins at the end," with Jesus's apocalyptic discussions of God's final intervention in human history and his own return as "the Son of Man." Participants will confront these challenging texts and find ways to interpret them that ready them to attend more faithfully to their neighbors' needs and struggles.

- Session 2: The Voice of John the Baptist—Advent continues with John the Baptist's calls in the wilderness to repentance and fresh beginnings in faithfulness. Participants will examine accounts of John's ministry and message from all four Gospels and consider ways in which they, like John, can testify to Jesus.

- Session 3: The Voices of Mary, Zechariah, and the Gospel of John—Poetic praise of God comes to the fore in Advent through the Magnificat of Mary, the Benedictus of Zechariah, and the elevated Prologue to John's Gospel. Participants will consider how these texts echo older voices and "older scripts" as they proclaim God's new activity in Jesus and will ponder their own imaginative images for Jesus's significance.
- Session 4: The Voices of Angels and Prophets—The stories of Jesus's birth in Matthew and Luke blend the ordinary and the extraordinary, the unremarkable and the remarkable. Participants will explore these familiar stories from what may be fresh perspectives and will identify signs of God's faithfulness that they, like those who first announced Jesus's coming, can offer to others.

Although this Leader Guide assumes all participants are reading *Voices of Advent*, its quotations from Matt's book and inclusion of key Scripture passages mean leaders can also use it on its own. Additionally, the accompanying DVD or streaming video from Amplify Media can supplement these session plans.

Each session contains the following elements to draw from as you plan four in-person, virtual, or hybrid sessions:

- Session Objectives
- Biblical Foundations—Key Scripture texts for each session, from the New Revised Standard Version, Updated Edition.
- Before Your Session—Tips to help you prepare a productive session.
- Starting Your Session—Discussion questions intended to "warm up" your group for fruitful discussion.

- Opening Prayer—Use the prayer as written or let it suggest a prayer in your own words.
- Book Discussion Questions—You likely will not be able or want to use all the questions in every session. Pick and choose questions based on your group's interests and the Spirit's leading.
- Closing Your Session—A discussion or reflection focused on a specific quotation from *Voices of Advent*.
- Closing Prayer—Each session suggests an Advent or Christmas hymn for use as a closing prayer.

Thank you for your willingness to lead! May you and your group find that these biblical voices of Advent encourage you to lift your own in praise of God and in witness to Jesus Christ all the year, for years to come.

SESSION 1

THE VOICE OF JESUS

SESSION GOALS

This session's reading, reflection, discussion, and prayer will help participants:

- Think about the extent to which their past and present experiences of Advent have focused on Jesus's past, present, and future comings.
- Understand, broadly, the history of the Advent season.
- Consider what "active, even insistent waiting" for God means and looks like.
- Interpret and appreciate Jesus's apocalyptic discussions of his future coming as the Son of Man in Mark 13, Matthew 24, and Luke 21.
- Identify ways in which hope for Jesus's return and attentiveness to God lead them and their congregations to attend to their neighbors' struggles and needs.

BIBLICAL FOUNDATIONS

[Jesus said,] "But in those days, after that suffering,

> *the sun will be darkened,*
> *and the moon will not give its light,*
> *and the stars will be falling from heaven,*
> *and the powers in the heavens will be shaken.*

"Then they will see 'the Son of Man coming in clouds' with great power and glory. Then he will send out the angels and gather the elect from the four winds, from the ends of the earth to the ends of heaven.

"From the fig tree learn its lesson: as soon as its branch becomes tender and puts forth its leaves, you know that summer is near. So also, when you see these things taking place, you know that he is near, at the very gates. Truly I tell you, this generation will not pass away until all these things have taken place. Heaven and earth will pass away, but my words will not pass away.

"But about that day or hour no one knows, neither the angels in heaven nor the Son, but only the Father. Beware, keep alert, for you do not know when the time will come. It is like a man going on a journey, when he leaves home and puts his slaves in charge, each with his work, and commands the doorkeeper to be on the watch. Therefore, keep awake, for you do not know when the master of the house will come, in the evening or at midnight or at cockcrow or at dawn, or else he may find you asleep when he comes suddenly. And what I say to you I say to all: Keep awake."

Mark 13:24-37

[Jesus said,] "But about that day and hour no one knows, neither the angels of heaven, nor the Son, but only the Father. For as the days of Noah were, so will be the coming of the Son of Man. For as in the days before the flood they were eating and drinking, marrying and giving in marriage, until the day Noah entered the ark, and they knew nothing until the flood came and swept them all away, so, too, will be the coming of the Son of Man. Then two will be in the field; one will be taken, and one will be left. Two women will be grinding meal together; one will be taken, and one will be left. Keep awake, therefore, for you do not know on what day your

Lord is coming. But understand this: if the owner of the house had known in what part of the night the thief was coming, he would have stayed awake and would not have let his house be broken into. Therefore you also must be ready, for the Son of Man is coming at an hour you do not expect."

Matthew 24:36-44

[Jesus said,] "There will be signs in the sun, the moon, and the stars and on the earth distress among nations confused by the roaring of the sea and the waves. People will faint from fear and foreboding of what is coming upon the world, for the powers of the heavens will be shaken. Then they will see 'the Son of Man coming in a cloud' with power and great glory. Now when these things begin to take place, stand up and raise your heads, because your redemption is drawing near."

Luke 21:25-28

BEFORE YOUR SESSION

- Carefully and prayerfully read this session's Biblical Foundations more than once. Note words and phrases that attract your attention and meditate on them. Write down questions you have, and try to answer them, consulting trusted Bible commentaries.
- Carefully read the Introduction and chapter 1 of *Voices of Advent* more than once.
- You will need: Bibles for in-person participants and/ or screen slides prepared with Scripture texts for sharing (identify the translation used); newsprint or a markerboard and markers (for in-person sessions); paper, pens or pencils (in-person).

- Prepare to distribute or display the discussion questions for small groups (see "The Son of Man Is Coming," pages 18–21).
- If using the DVD or streaming video, preview the session 1 video segment. Choose the best time in your session plan for viewing it.

STARTING YOUR SESSION

Welcome participants. Express why you are enthusiastic about leading this study of *Voices of Advent*. Invite participants to talk briefly about what they hope to gain from the study.

Ask:

- When each year do you start decorating for Christmas or listening to Christmas music? Why?
- How much distinction between Christmas and Advent do you draw? How much distinction does your congregation draw?
- Do you have a favorite *Advent*-specific tradition? If so, what is it, and why?
- How would you answer someone who asked, "What's the Advent season all about?"

Review these points:

- *Advent* means "arrival" or "coming" (from Latin *adventus*).
- Advent focuses on Jesus's coming as a baby (in history), in our present experience (in mystery), and when God makes all things new (in majesty).
- Advent was originally a fast to prepare for the feast of Christmas.

- Pope Gregory I (died 604) set Advent's length as four weeks; previously, churches in different places observed it for different lengths of time.
- Although Christians did not widely observe Christmas until the fourth century, Christian authors as early as Justin Martyr (died circa 165 CE, one of the early church's most important philosophers and theologians) understood a connection between Jesus's birth and future return.

Read aloud from Matt's book: "[O]ur Christian ancestors through the centuries have found value in treating the season [of Advent] as more than a countdown to December 25.... By turning our attention to Jesus's presence—past, present, and future—Advent infuses in us Christ-centered perspectives about God's commitment to the world and about the meaning of our lives."

Discuss:

- Thinking about past experiences of Advent, where has the season's emphasis mostly fallen for you: Jesus's past coming, continued presence, or future coming? Why?
- How, if at all, would you like to experience Advent differently, and why?

Opening Prayer

Almighty God, who is and who was and is coming, you have promised a new reality is on the way, a reality in which all life flourishes as you created it to. In the birth of Jesus, you have proven your faithfulness and your will to be with us. As we study your Word in this season of waiting, may your Spirit move us to more fully trust your commitment to us and to the world by more fully entrusting ourselves to you. **Amen.**

WATCH SESSION VIDEO

Watch the session 1 video segment together. Discuss:

- Which of Matt's statements most interested, intrigued, surprised, or confused you? Why?
- What questions does this video segment raise for you?

WAITING FOR GOD TO SHOW UP

Talk briefly about a time you waited for something. Invite volunteers to talk briefly about a memorable experience of waiting. Ask:

- When and why can waiting be easy? When and why can it be difficult?
- Do you think of waiting as mostly passive or mostly active? Why?
- How much trouble, if any, did you have waiting for Christmas when you were younger? How, if at all, is waiting for Christmas different now, and why?
- How is waiting for *Christ* different than waiting for *Christmas*?

Read aloud from Matt's book: "Advent is a season of waiting, but it's not a season of pointless waiting. . . . In Advent we extol the importance of active, even insistent waiting. . . . The church grows fidgety, expecting something to happen. We're asking God to show up. Actually, we're imploring God."

Discuss:

- When, if ever, did you ask or implore God to show up? What happened?

- What does "active, even insistent waiting" for God look like, specifically?

- Matt says one form of active waiting is "internal housecleaning"—taking stock of and owning up to our shortcomings. When was a time you recognized, willingly or unwillingly, a shortcoming? What did this recognition lead you to do? To what extent is this kind of introspection a regular part of your spiritual practice?

- Matt says Advent's "call to introspection is not the same thing as the church trying to be a moral scold or aiming to make people feel bad about themselves. It's about raising the stakes." When, if ever, have you experienced moral scolding from the church? How did you respond? How can faith communities encourage "internal housecleaning" without falling into moral scolding? How can they take stock of their own shortcomings as institutions?

- Matt quotes an Advent sermon by Dietrich Bonhoeffer in which Bonhoeffer calls God's coming "frightening news for everyone who has a conscience" before it is good news, claiming we can only recognize the "incomparable kindness" of God's coming after experiencing its potential terror. Do you agree? Why or why not?

- Active, insistent Advent waiting "entails a hunger to see things change and a willingness to get involved." When considering the world's shortcomings, where do you hunger most for things to change? How are you involved in efforts to make those changes?

- "Christian hope is more about confident expectation than it is about optimism or wishful thinking, because hope is a product of the trustworthiness that God has already demonstrated to us." To what evidence for confident hope

in God does Advent point? How, if at all, does this evidence
give you courage to make yourself available for God's work?

- "God wants to be with us. God will be with us. Those
  are massive claims that should cause us to reassess our
  tremendous value in God's estimation." How does God's
  will to be with humanity shape the way you think and feel
  about other people? About yourself?

PAROUSIA AND APOCALYPSE

Write the words *parousia* and *apocalypse* on newsprint or a
markerboard.

Define *parousia* (pah-roo-SEE-uh) as a Greek word meaning
"arrival" or "appearance." Not new in or unique to the New Testament,
it could mean "the manifestation of a god or, more commonly, a visit
from a dignitary." Ask participants if they have ever seen a dignitary's
parousia. Point out that a *parousia* is highly visible. The New Testament
frequently calls Jesus's future return his *parousia*.

Ask participants what they think when they hear the word
apocalypse. Define it as a word, from the Greek *apokalupsis*, which
means not a spectacular disaster but "a revelation or an uncovering"
of something previously unknown.

Tell participants *apocalypse* also refers to a kind of Jewish literature
that flourished during the second century BCE and the first century
CE. Apocalyptic literature uses often dramatic symbolism to assert
God's command of history despite the difficulties and conflicts
people face. It proclaims "God is about to break in and set the
world to rights," as Matt writes. The Bible does not contain much
apocalyptic literature—Daniel 7–12 and Revelation are the major
examples—but an apocalyptic worldview was familiar to Jesus and
his first followers.

THE SON OF MAN IS COMING

Tell participants that Matthew, Mark, and Luke all preserve traditions about Jesus discussing his future return as "the Son of Man" ("the Human One," "the Son of Humanity"). Recruit a volunteer to read aloud Daniel 7:9-14. Discuss:

- What does the "one like a son of man" (Daniel 7:13; "like a human being," NRSVue) in Daniel's apocalyptic vision do? What does this figure's coming mean for the world?
- What kinds of expectations and emotions might have been stirred up by this title when Jesus's earliest followers applied it to him?

Form three groups of participants. Assign each group one of these scriptures to read and discuss: Mark 13:24-37; Matthew 24:29-44; Luke 21:25-36. Tell participants all three scriptures:

- Take place a few days before the Passover, after Jesus has entered Jerusalem and has had several confrontations with the Temple leadership. Some of these leaders will hand him over to Pontius Pilate, the Roman governor of Judea, who will order his crucifixion.
- Follow people talking about their awestruck admiration of the Temple—"an eye-popping architectural accomplishment adorned with precious metals and jewels." Jesus foretells the Temple's destruction, which occurred in 70 CE, when the Roman Empire put down a revolt among Jews in Judea (66–70 CE).
- Are part of Jesus's response to questions about when the Temple's destruction will happen, although he doesn't answer those questions narrowly or directly; instead, he is "describing larger and recurring patterns of peril and conflict in the world."

Have the three small groups read their assigned scripture and discuss these questions about it, which you should distribute or display for participants' ease of reference:

- What signs accompany the Son of Man's appearance, and what do these signs mean?
- What does the Son of Man do when he appears?
- What does Jesus say about when the Son of Man will come?
- What instructions does Jesus give?

After allowing 10–20 minutes for reading and discussion, bring all groups together. Invite a volunteer from each group to report on the highlights of their small group's discussion.

Use some of these questions to lead a discussion about these three scriptures similarities, differences, and distinctive content:

- What do you hear Jesus saying in all these scriptures? How would you sum up his message in these passages?
- What do these scriptures leave you thinking and feeling?
- According to Matt, the cosmic disruptions Jesus describes are not "predictive signs" but "confirmations of Jesus's power and identity." How so? What do signs in the heavens indicate about how Jesus's future *parousia* will differ from his past or present comings?
- "Today," Matt writes, "we have explanations for phenomena such as changes in the heavens, earthquakes, and violent weather." Do these explanations weaken or invalidate these symbols' force or significance? Why or why not?
- Why, in Luke 21:28, does Jesus tell his followers to "stand up and raise [their] heads" in the face of cosmic signs of upheaval? Does his instruction encourage a lack of engagement in times of distress and suffering? Why or why not?

- Why does Jesus compare watching for signs of his coming to observing a fig tree?
- How do you understand Jesus's statement that "this generation" will experience the Son of Man's coming (Mark 13:30; Matthew 24:34; Luke 21:32)?
- In Matthew 24:36, Jesus says "only the Father" knows the timing of his return. How, if at all, does this statement relate to his earlier lesson from the fig tree? How does or how ought it shape Christians' interest in and response to efforts to predict when Jesus will return?
- In Matthew 24:37-39, why does Jesus compare the time of his future coming to the time of Noah? What, if anything, does his emphasis on what Matt calls "humanity's normal affairs" suggest about what Jesus's followers ought to be doing while waiting for his return, and how they ought to be doing it?
- In Matthew 24:40-41, Jesus talks about a future sorting, a recurring theme in Matthew's Gospel (for example, 13:24-30, 36-43; 25:1-13, 31-46). As Matt notes, "Jesus doesn't specify whether it's better to be left or taken.... [This passage is] not a diagram of the afterlife." If, as Matt states, Jesus isn't talking about a "rapture," what is he talking about, and why?
- Matt explains that dualistic thinking, like that in Matthew 24:40-41, is common in apocalyptic worldviews. What purposes can such thinking serve? What problems can it create? When, if ever, have you encountered it? How do and ought Christians respond to it?
- Although other scriptures talk about wrath and judgment in connection with God's future intervention in history, these scriptures do not. What, if anything, does this fact suggest about the significance of Jesus's return as the Son of Man?

- Matt suggests that Jesus's discussion of his future return after "strife and terror" intimates "the powers of this world that wreck lives and the creation (that is, the world's systems, hatreds, fears, oppressors, and more) are not absolute. They will not last forever." Do you find that message in these Scriptures? Why or why not?
- "[T]he church rediscovers its true purpose when things are at their worst." Do you agree? Why or why not?
- Matt also states that Jesus gives "no explicit promise of a new state of affairs, only the promise of a coming person: Jesus himself. . . . Before Advent is hope for any*thing*, it is hope for Jesus." What difference does it make to you that the object of Advent hope is in the person of Jesus and not, as Matt says, "in ideals, statistics, or policies"?

CLOSING YOUR SESSION

Remind participants that in the Scriptures you all have explored in this session, Jesus calls his disciples to be alert and to pay attention. Suggest he calls disciples today to pay attention to more than possible signs of his *parousia*.

Read aloud from Matt's book: "Attentiveness to God will produce attentiveness to our neighbors. Attentiveness to our neighbors will produce attentiveness to their needs and struggles, even as it produces appreciation for who they are as people made in God's image."

Discuss:

- How does paying attention to God lead us to pay more attention to other people?
- How does hope for Jesus's future return inspire and sustain attentive care for other people and for the world today?
- What are some specific ways you and your congregation are paying attention to your neighbors' struggles and needs in this Advent season?

CLOSING PRAYER

Sing (or read aloud) together at least these verses of "O Lord, How Shall I Meet You?" (Paul Gerhardt, 1653; translated by Catherine Winkworth; https://hymnary.org/text/o_lord_how_shall_i_meet_thee), which speak to Jesus's comings in history, mystery, and majesty:

O Lord, how shall I meet You,
how welcome You aright?
Your people long to greet You,
my Hope, my heart's Delight!
O, kindle, Lord most holy,
Your lamp within my breast
to do in spirit lowly
all that may please You best.

Love caused Your incarnation;
love brought You down to me.
Your thirst for my salvation
procured my liberty.
O, love beyond all telling,
that led You to embrace
in love, all love excelling,
our lost and fallen race.

He comes to judge the nations,
a terror to His foes,
a light of consolations
and blessed hope to those
who love the Lord's appearing.
O glorious Sun, now come,
send forth Your beams most cheering
and guide us safely home.

SESSION 2

THE VOICE OF
JOHN THE BAPTIST

SESSION GOALS

This session's reading, reflection, discussion, and prayer will help participants:

- Understand key elements of John the Baptist's life and work.
- Compare and contrast the four Gospels' presentations of John, attending to ways each one emphasizes distinct aspects of his ministry, message, and significance.
- Consider how the story of John's question of Jesus (Matthew 11:2-6) addresses Christians' "in-between" experience of faith.
- Identify specific actions they can take to testify to Jesus, the true Light (John 1:8-9).

BIBLICAL FOUNDATIONS

The beginning of the good news of Jesus Christ.

As it is written in the prophet Isaiah,

> *"See, I am sending my messenger ahead of you,*
> *who will prepare your way,*

the voice of one crying out in the wilderness:
  'Prepare the way of the Lord;
  make his paths straight,'"

so John the baptizer appeared in the wilderness, proclaiming a baptism of repentance for the forgiveness of sins. And the whole Judean region and all the people of Jerusalem were going out to him and were baptized by him in the River Jordan, confessing their sins. Now John was clothed with camel's hair, with a leather belt around his waist, and he ate locusts and wild honey. He proclaimed, "The one who is more powerful than I is coming after me; I am not worthy to stoop down and untie the strap of his sandals. I have baptized you with water, but he will baptize you with the Holy Spirit."

Mark 1:1-8

[John said,] "Even now the ax is lying at the root of the trees; therefore every tree that does not bear good fruit will be cut down and thrown into the fire.

"I baptize you with water for repentance, but the one who is coming after me is more powerful than I, and I am not worthy to carry his sandals. He will baptize you with the Holy Spirit and fire. His winnowing fork is in his hand, and he will clear his threshing floor and will gather his wheat into the granary, but the chaff he will burn with unquenchable fire."

Matthew 3:10-12

And the crowds asked [John], "What, then, should we do?" In reply he said to them, "Whoever has two coats must share with anyone who has none, and whoever has food must do likewise." Even tax collectors came to be baptized, and they asked him, "Teacher, what should we do?" He said to them, "Collect no more than the amount prescribed for you." Soldiers also asked him, "And we, what should we do?" He said to them, "Do not extort money from anyone by threats or false accusation, and be satisfied with your wages."

Luke 3:10-14

There was a man sent from God whose name was John. He came as a witness to testify to the light, so that all might believe through him. He himself was not the light, but he came to testify to the light. The true light, which enlightens everyone, was coming into the world....

The next day [John] saw Jesus coming toward him and declared, "Here is the Lamb of God who takes away the sin of the world!"

John 1:6-9, 29

When John heard in prison what the Messiah was doing, he sent word by his disciples and said to him, "Are you the one who is to come, or are we to wait for another?" Jesus answered them, "Go and tell John what you hear and see: the blind receive their sight, the lame walk, those with a skin disease are cleansed, the deaf hear, the dead are raised, and the poor have good news brought to them. And blessed is anyone who takes no offense at me."

Matthew 11:2-6

BEFORE YOUR SESSION

- Carefully and prayerfully read this session's Biblical Foundations more than once. Note words and phrases that attract your attention and meditate on them. Write down questions you have and try to answer them, consulting trusted Bible commentaries.
- Carefully read chapter 2 of *Voices of Advent* more than once.
- You will need: Bibles for in-person participants and/ or screen slides prepared with scripture texts for sharing

(identify the translation used); newsprint or a markerboard and markers (for in-person sessions); paper, pens or pencils (in-person); wax or electric votive candles (*optional*).

- Locate at least one image of the Isenheim Altarpiece (1512-1516) by Matthias Grünewald that you can display during your session.
- If using the DVD or streaming video, preview the session 2 video segment. Choose the best time in your session plan for viewing it.

STARTING YOUR SESSION

Welcome participants. Display the image(s) of the Isenheim Altarpiece (a painting designed to be displayed behind an altar) you chose before your session. Invite volunteers to comment on what details in the art most draw and hold their attention and why, and to talk briefly about what the art leads them to think and feel.

Point out (if no one else has) the figure of John the Baptist who, as Matt writes, is "holding a book, and pointing a rather long index finger straight at Jesus's corpse." Next to John are the words, in Latin, "He must increase, but I must decrease" (John 3:30). (You may not be able to see the text unless looking at a close-up detail photo.) The cross-carrying lamb next to John represents how John called Jesus "the Lamb of God" (John 1:29, 36). Discuss:

- Why is this art, as Matt says, an "accurate visual summary of the main thing that the New Testament writers want you to know about John the Baptist"?
- As Matt notes, John wasn't present at Jesus's crucifixion, having been executed before Jesus was. Why has the artist included John in this scene?

- Although John told people to expect someone "more powerful" than he was to come, "[h]anging on a cross is about the most powerless posture one can imagine. . . . Sometimes God's arrival and God's power don't match what we might expect." When, if ever, have you been surprised to discover God's presence and power in unexpected places or people?
- "People like John," writes Matt, "urge us to examine everything more closely." Who is someone who urged you to examine something or someone more closely for evidence of God's presence or activity? How did they do so? What, if anything, did you see upon closer examination?
- When, if ever, have you urged someone else to examine someone or something more closely for glimpses of God? What happened?

OPENING PRAYER

Holy God, you sent your servant John to prepare your people for the Savior. Send your Spirit upon us now, we pray, as we study his ministry and listen to his message. Move us to know and do your will with urgency, as John sought to know and do it, that we may more clearly see your salvation bringing mountains low and making rough places plain, in this world and in our lives. **Amen.**

WATCH SESSION VIDEO

Watch the session 2 video segment together. Discuss:

- Which of Matt's statements most interested, intrigued, surprised, or confused you? Why?
- What questions does this video segment raise for you?

MEETING JOHN THE BAPTIST

Lead participants in brainstorming a list of everything they know or can remember about John the Baptist. Write responses on newsprint or a markerboard. As needed, supplement the brainstorming and discussion with these points:

- He was born to Zechariah the priest and Elizabeth, his wife, when both were old and had been unable to conceive children (Luke 1:5-25, 57-66).

- Only Luke's Gospel tells the story of John's birth, closely connecting it with the story of Jesus's birth (1:36, 39-45). In Matthew, Mark, and John, John the Baptist first appears as an adult, preaching and baptizing in the wilderness near the Jordan River, circa 27-29 CE.

- Only Luke mentions a family relationship between Jesus's and John's mothers (Gabriel calls Elizabeth Mary's "relative," 1:36).

- John likely saw himself as a reformer, practicing his form of baptism as an alternative to similar purification rituals in water that were associated with the Temple in Jerusalem.

- Baptism (from the Greek *baptizō*, "to immerse, to dip") was not unique to John in first-century Judaism. The first-century Jewish historian Josephus says John baptized to purify bodies; the Gospels tend to describe it as a "baptism of repentance."

- John "probably influenced Jesus and his message"—both preached about the nearness of God's kingdom; Jesus's disciples also baptized (according to John 3:22; 4:1-2); and Jesus may have echoed some of John's criticisms of elite Temple leadership.

- Herod Antipas (son of the Christmas story's "King Herod," Herod the Great) had John arrested and beheaded (Mark 6:14-29; Matthew 14:1-12; Luke 3:18-20; 9:7-9) because, according to the Gospels, John criticized Herod's marriage to Herodias (his brother's wife).

- Josephus confirms John's popularity and says Herod Antipas executed John because he feared John and John's followers could spark an insurrection.

- John may have been aligned with groups of Essenes, first-century Jewish communities living in the wilderness, some of whom had soured on the Temple because of its leadership. The most famous Essene community produced the Dead Sea Scrolls, which include expectations "that God would soon purge the world of wickedness and usher in a new era of righteousness."

JOHN IN THE GOSPELS

Recruit a volunteer to read aloud Mark 1:1-8. Discuss:

- Why does Mark begin "the good news of Jesus Christ" (verse 1) with a report about John the Baptist?

- Read these scriptures: Isaiah 40:1-5; Exodus 23:20-21; Malachi 3:1-4. How does Mark "blend" these scriptures in verses 2-3? How can these scriptures help us understand the "way" John prepares?

- What other biblical stories about God and God's people in the wilderness do you remember? What personal experiences, if any, do you have of being in a wilderness? How do these stories and experiences inform your understanding of the setting for John's ministry?

- Do you agree with Matt that "God tends to show up in out-of-the-way places and out-of-the-way processes"? Do you think Jesus confirms this divine tendency? Why or why not? In what out-of-the-way places or processes, if any, have you encountered God?
- John's clothing (verse 6) resembles that of the important prophet Elijah (2 Kings 1:8). How does Malachi 4:5-6 reflect some Jewish expectations about Elijah's place in God's plans and promises for the future? Why might John have styled his appearance after Elijah's?
- Who and what does John tell those who come to be baptized to expect after him (verses 7-8)? What do you think John means, and why?

Recruit a volunteer to read aloud Matthew 3:1-12. Discuss:

- How is Matthew's account of John's ministry like and unlike Mark's?
- Why does John criticize the religious leaders who come to him for baptism (verses 7-9)? Why is it important to remember John is a devout Jew critiquing other devout Jews? How, if at all, have you encountered the attitudes John denounces in your own religious tradition?
- Do you respond positively or negatively to the word *repentance*? Why?
- As Matt explains, the word for *repentance* in New Testament Greek (*metanoia*, meh-tuh-NOY-uh) "does not refer to contrition or feeling self-blaming regret about one's behavior" but to "taking on a new perspective or a changed mind." How, if at all, does this definition affect your response to calls for repentance?

- Matt says John urges people "to perceive the great discrepancy between how things are and how things ought to be, in God's merciful assessment of our reality." Do you hear mercy in John's message? Why or why not? How can knowing and telling the truth about the gap between "what is" and "what ought to be" be a mercy?

- Matt refers to Bryan Stevenson's argument that we cannot repair injustices without first engaging in confession. When have you seen or participated in confession that helped lead to justice?

- John's "urgency and warnings reveal his exasperation about a society that isn't living up to what it can be or is being held back from being what it can be." In what areas of your society do you share John's dissatisfaction with the world as it is? How, if at all, are you turning that dissatisfaction and exasperation into action?

- John's images of the coming one's "winnowing fork" and "unquenchable fire" (verse 12) make clear, as Matt writes, that "any judgment that's going to happen is Jesus's responsibility and not John's or anyone else's." How can this truth help us keep what we say and do to effect change in proper perspective?

Recruit a volunteer to read aloud Luke 3:1-18. Discuss:

- How is Luke's account of John's ministry like and unlike Mark's and Matthew's?

- Why does Luke take time to situate John in a wider historical and political context (verses 1-2)?

- Matt states that "faithfulness is made up of daily actions and regular choices. Change and compassion begin there." How do John's instructions to the crowds (verses 10-11) illustrate this idea?

- Tax collectors and soldiers worked for the Roman Empire, with "great latitude in being able to exploit their positions for personal gain," Matt notes. What do you think about John's instructions to them (verses 12-14)? What do you imagine others in the crowd thought about what John told the tax collectors and soldiers, and why?
- "John's not paralyzed by the magnitude of what we call structural or systemic injustice. He calls for resisting it through basic decency and faithfulness." What are some specific ways in which you demonstrate basic decency and faithfulness? Do you tend to think of these actions as part of your discipleship? Why or why not?
- "Advent and the promise of Christ's coming involve an invitation to enlist ourselves in his cause not by completing a long moral checklist but by looking out for our neighbors, especially the ones who have been denied opportunities to enjoy their basic dignity." Who are these neighbors for you? for your congregation? How, specifically, are you looking out for them?
- Why do you think the crowds wonder "whether [John] might be the Messiah" (verse 15)?

Recruit volunteers to read aloud John 1:6-9, 19-28, 29-34. Discuss:

- What is John's main mission, according to this Gospel (verses 6-8)? How does baptizing activity support this mission (verse 31)?
- Why do the religious leaders question John about who he is (verses 19-23)? How do John's answers further his mission?
- How is the way in which John talks about his relationship to Jesus (verses 26-27, 30-33) like and unlike how he talks about it in the other Gospels?

- Why do you think this Gospel, unlike the others, does not include or refer to a scene of Jesus being baptized?
- In the Fourth Gospel, says Matt, "John the Baptist's voice offers a statement of certainty: We've found our Messiah." When, if ever, have you felt such certainty about someone and who they are to you? Who, if anyone, has declared to you who Jesus is with such certainty? Have you ever felt such certainty about Jesus yourself? Why or why not?
- Only John's Gospel calls Jesus "the Lamb of God who takes away the sin of the world" (verse 29). Matt explains that the Passover lamb, to which this title alludes, "was not considered a payment or a sacrifice for sin but a means by which God claims God's people and rescues them from oppression" (see Exodus 12:21-27). When and how, if at all, have you or those you know of experienced Jesus as liberating from oppression?
- In this Gospel, John the Baptist not only knows who Jesus is but also points others to him. What have you and your congregation done, and what do you do now, to direct others' attention to Jesus?

"ARE YOU THE ONE?"

Recruit a volunteer to read aloud Matthew 11:2-6. Discuss:

- Why do you think John wanted to ask Jesus this question? Have you ever asked, or wanted to ask, the same question of Jesus? Why?
- Matthew does not tell us what John thought about Jesus's answer. What do you think about it?
- Matt calls Jesus's activity "a reckoning of sorts." How so? How, if at all, do you see this activity occurring today, and would you attribute it to Jesus? Why or why not?

- How does Jesus continue to confound Christians' expectations about who "the Messiah" (verse 2) should be and what the Messiah should do?

- How can this story about John's question help us "live on the brink," in Matt's words—in the "in-betweenness" of God's promises on the one hand and our experience of the world on the other?

- "On one side, John the visionary gives voice to expectations that can agitate us and make us eager to spring into action.... On the other side, Jesus, especially in the message he sends back to answer John's questions, reminds us that we follow *him* and stay attentive to where and how he leads. He's changing the world, but it's his road that we're walking.... [and] the road can't skirt the cross ahead." How, specifically, do we stay attentive to where and how Jesus leads us?

CLOSING YOUR SESSION

Read aloud from Matt's book: "Those candles on the [Advent] wreaths do more than provide stubborn resistance against encroaching shadows. Flames in the Bible symbolize purification and wholeness. Moreover, they symbolize God's presence. The tiny fires contain more power than they appear to, for they become to me a lighthouse of that active hope, vaguely illuminating in my mind a future that I'm still trying to see."

Distribute wax or electric votive candles (optional). Ask participants to think about an "encroaching shadow" that concerns them, as well as some specific action they can take to light a "tiny fire" against it. Remind participants that, as we saw in Luke's presentation of John the Baptist, grand and heroic actions are not always what God requires; small actions, too, can be "fruits of repentance." Invite volunteers to respond to the prompt aloud, lighting their candle as they do (*optional*).

Say: "Like John, we ourselves are not the light, but we are called to testify to the true Light, who enlightens everyone, who is coming into the world."

CLOSING PRAYER

Sing (or read aloud) together "Come, Thou Long-Expected Jesus" (Charles Wesley, 1744; https://hymnary.org/text/come_thou_long _expected_jesus_born_to), which, as did John, identifies Jesus as the one born to be the hope of God's people and the world for freedom:

Come, thou long expected Jesus,
born to set thy people free;
from our fears and sins release us,
let us find our rest in thee.
Israel's strength and consolation,
hope of all the earth thou art;
dear desire of every nation,
joy of every longing heart.

Born thy people to deliver,
born a child and yet a King,
born to reign in us forever,
now thy gracious kingdom bring.
By thine own eternal spirit
rule in all our hearts alone;
by thine all sufficient merit,
raise us to thy glorious throne.

SESSION 3

THE VOICES OF MARY, ZECHARIAH, AND THE GOSPEL OF JOHN

SESSION GOALS

This session's reading, reflection, discussion, and prayer will help participants:

- Reflect on experiences of drawing on "old scripts" and echoing "older voices" when they seek to understand and communicate new experiences and insights.
- Consider Gabriel's announcement to Mary (Luke 1:26-38) in the context of notable Old Testament "annunciations" as well as Mary's consent to God's will as a model for our own.
- Ponder how the songs of Mary (1:46b-55) and Zechariah (1:68-79) connect to God's past with God's people while proclaiming new things God is doing, and think about these songs' ethical implications for Christians today.
- Explore how the language of the Prologue to John (John 1:1-18) uses biblical, philosophical, and poetic language to communicate Jesus's significance.
- Exercise their imaginations in choosing or creating a poetic image for God and/or Jesus.

BIBLICAL FOUNDATIONS

In the sixth month [of Elizabeth's pregnancy] the angel Gabriel was sent by God to a town in Galilee called Nazareth, to a virgin engaged to a man whose name was Joseph, of the house of David. The virgin's name was Mary. And he came to her and said, "Greetings, favored one! The Lord is with you." But she was much perplexed by his words and pondered what sort of greeting this might be. The angel said to her, "Do not be afraid, Mary, for you have found favor with God. And now, you will conceive in your womb and bear a son, and you will name him Jesus. He will be great and will be called the Son of the Most High, and the Lord God will give to him the throne of his ancestor David. He will reign over the house of Jacob forever, and of his kingdom there will be no end." Mary said to the angel, "How can this be, since I am a virgin?" The angel said to her, "The Holy Spirit will come upon you, and the power of the Most High will overshadow you; therefore the child to be born will be holy; he will be called Son of God. And now, your relative Elizabeth in her old age has also conceived a son, and this is the sixth month for her who was said to be barren. For nothing will be impossible with God." Then Mary said, "Here am I, the servant of the Lord; let it be with me according to your word." Then the angel departed from her.

Luke 1:26-38

My soul magnifies the Lord,
*   and my spirit rejoices in God my Savior,*
for he has looked with favor on the lowly state of his servant.
*   Surely from now on all generations will call me blessed,*
for the Mighty One has done great things for me,
*   and holy is his name;*
indeed, his mercy is for those who fear him

from generation to generation.
He has shown strength with his arm;
 he has scattered the proud in the imagination of their hearts.
He has brought down the powerful from their thrones
 and lifted up the lowly;
he has filled the hungry with good things
 and sent the rich away empty.
He has come to the aid of his child Israel,
 in remembrance of his mercy,
according to the promise he made to our ancestors,
 to Abraham and to his descendants forever.

         Luke 1:46b-55

Blessed be the Lord God of Israel,
 for he has looked favorably on his people and redeemed them.
He has raised up a mighty savior for us
 in the house of his child David,
as he spoke through the mouth of his holy prophets from of old,
 that we would be saved from our enemies and from the hand of
 all who hate us.
Thus he has shown the mercy promised to our ancestors
 and has remembered his holy covenant,
the oath that he swore to our ancestor Abraham,
to grant us that we, being rescued from the hands of our enemies,
might serve him without fear, in holiness and righteousness
 in his presence all our days.
And you, child, will be called the prophet of the Most High,
 for you will go before the Lord to prepare his ways,
to give his people knowledge of salvation
 by the forgiveness of their sins.
Because of the tender mercy of our God,
 the dawn from on high will break upon us,

to shine upon those who sit in darkness and in the shadow of death,
to guide our feet into the way of peace."

Luke 1:68-79

In the beginning was the Word, and the Word was with God, and the Word was God. He was in the beginning with God. All things came into being through him, and without him not one thing came into being. What has come into being in him was life, and the life was the light of all people. The light shines in the darkness, and the darkness did not overtake it....

And the Word became flesh and lived among us, and we have seen his glory, the glory as of a father's only son, full of grace and truth.... From his fullness we have all received, grace upon grace. The law indeed was given through Moses; grace and truth came through Jesus Christ. No one has ever seen God. It is the only Son, himself God, who is close to the Father's heart, who has made him known.

John 1:1-5, 14, 16-18

BEFORE YOUR SESSION

- Carefully and prayerfully read this session's Biblical Foundations more than once. Note words and phrases that attract your attention and meditate on them. Write down questions you have and try to answer them, consulting trusted Bible commentaries.
- Carefully read chapter 3 of *Voices of Advent* more than once.
- You will need: Bibles for in-person participants and/ or screen slides prepared with scripture texts for sharing (identify the translation used); newsprint or a markerboard and markers (for in-person sessions); paper, pens or pencils (in-person). *Optional*: newspapers and magazines (see "Closing Your Session").

- If using the DVD or streaming video, preview the session 3 video segment. Choose the best time in your session plan for viewing it.

- *Optional*: Choose recordings of musical settings of the Magnificat and the Benedictus to play during your session, or choose hymns or songs based on these texts to sing together.

STARTING YOUR SESSION

Welcome participants. Ask:

- When was a time you caught yourself sounding like your parents or another important adult from your past, as Matt has caught himself sounding like his parents?

- What's an old saying—from your family, history, popular culture, or elsewhere—you find yourself quoting often, and why?

- What are possible advantages of relying on "old scripts" when trying to process and communicate new experiences and insights? What are possible disadvantages?

Read aloud from Matt's book: "The authors who wrote the Gospels could have composed stories to depict the coming of Jesus as something entirely unprecedented or even the work of a new or different deity....As the Gospels talk about God and the arrival of Jesus as a manifestation of God's intentions, they remind us that nothing is entirely new."

Tell participants that, in this session, your group will explore how the Advent voices of Mary, Zechariah, and the Gospel of John follow "old scripts" and echo "older voices" as they bear witness to God's activity in Jesus's birth; and how these older scripts and voices can "help us discover something new."

OPENING PRAYER

Eternal God, throughout the ages you have summoned faithful voices to proclaim your power, prophesy about your truth, sing your goodness, and marvel at your love. We thank you for the great chorus of believers who have spoken and sung your praise, and ask that, by your Spirit, you would strengthen us in this study to raise our voices with theirs, joining the festal shout they raise to your Word made flesh, Jesus Christ. **Amen.**

WATCH SESSION VIDEO

Watch the session 3 video segment together. Discuss:

- Which of Matt's statements most interested, intrigued, surprised, or confused you? Why?
- What questions does this video segment raise for you?

THE ANNUNCIATION

Recruit three volunteers to read aloud Luke 1:26-38, as the narrator, the angel Gabriel, and Mary. Discuss:

- Matt points out "Christian tradition remembers [this scene] as 'the Annunciation.'" If you were giving this story a title, what would you call it, and why?
- Miraculous announcements of unlikely pregnancies occur more than once in the story of God and God's people. Read one or more of these scriptures: Genesis 18:1-15; Judges 13:2-23; 1 Samuel 1:1-18. What connections can you make between these birth announcements and the announcement of Jesus's birth? How do they help you understand the story in Luke 1?

- How does Gabriel reference God's past with the people in his message to Mary (verses 32-33)? How does 2 Samuel 7:4-16 connect to Gabriel's words? What do these connections tell us about both God and the people?
- How is Mary's response to Gabriel in verse 34 like and/ or unlike Zechariah's response to Gabriel in Luke 1:18? Matt amusingly speculates that Gabriel may have made Zechariah mute "to avoid a prolonged argument with him"—what do you think? What, if anything, distinguishes unwelcome questions of God from welcome ones, unacceptable questions from acceptable?
- Matt writes, "Focusing on Mary's consent [to God's plan for Jesus's birth] is essential." Do you think Mary could have said "no" to this message? What do you imagine would have happened if she had? Why is it "especially important" to note and appreciate Mary's consent "[i]n our own cultural landscape," as Matt states?
- How does viewing Mary as more than "God-bearer" (one of her traditional titles) help us appreciate her and her role as Jesus's mother more fully?
- "The story of Jesus's birth remains a story of divine initiative, but Mary's consent reminds us that human contributions also play a part." Why does God choose to invite and involve human contributions in accomplishing God's will? When and how, if ever, do you believe you and your congregation have made valuable human contributions to an action God initiated?
- How does or how could Mary's consent to God's will inspire or inform your own decisions to say "yes" to what God asks of you?

- Gabriel tells Mary "nothing will be impossible with God" (verse 37)—"a sentence," Matt writes, "that encapsulates the whole message of Advent and Christmas well." Do you agree? Why or why not? How easy or difficult do you find Gabriel's statement to accept? Why?

MARY'S PROPHETIC PRAISE

Recruit a volunteer to read aloud Luke 1:46b-55, Mary's speech/song/prayer traditionally called the Magnificat (after the first word in its Latin translation). Discuss:

- What word or image in Mary's speech most captures your attention or imagination? Why?
- Mary "speaks as a prophet," writes Matt, "for she describes who this emerging story of the Messiah within her is about and explains where it is headed." How would you summarize what she has to say about this "who" and "where"?
- "Instead of reciting God's résumé of discrete accomplishments, Mary offers a character sketch." What adjectives describe God's character, as Mary presents it? How do you respond to her "character sketch" of God?
- "Whatever [Mary] perceives about the future her son will bring about, it looks familiar to her, given what she and her ancestors already have learned about God." How does Mary's message connect to God's past history with the people? What do these connections tell us about both God and the people?
- Read 1 Samuel 2:1-10. How are Hannah's and Mary's prayers alike and unalike? What significance do you find in these similarities and differences?

- Read Luke 6:20-26. How does Jesus's vision of God's values mirror his mother's? What other ways can you think of in which Jesus, as Matt says, is "out to reorder the values, privileges, and blessings" societies bestow on some people at other, so-called "lesser" people's expense?
- "The song is about God," Matt reminds us, "not a political party or a list of economic policies we might want to ascribe to God." What makes confusing or conflating God with human political, economic, and social aims a persistent temptation? How can and do we guard against it?
- "The story that [Mary's] song tells about God begins in her own experience. . . . Mary describes God, first, by asserting what she knows in herself to be true about God." How often do you begin your talk about God in your own experience? Why? Do we ever need to begin our talk about God from some other source? Why or why not?
- How does listening to other people's experience of and assertions about God, both past and present, help us clarify and correct our own?
- What actions, if any, do you think Mary's song calls Christians today to take, and why?

Optional: Play a recording of a musical setting of the Magnificat, or sing together a hymn or song based on the text. Briefly discuss how the music affects what participants hear in and through the text.

ZECHARIAH'S PROPHETIC PRAISE

Recruit a volunteer to read aloud Luke 1:68-79, Zechariah's speech/song/prayer traditionally called the Benedictus (after the first word in its Latin translation). Discuss:

- What word or image in Zechariah's speech most captures your attention or imagination? Why?

- How is Zechariah's song like and unlike Mary's song? What significance do you find in these similarities and differences?
- "Zechariah, very much a product of his Jewish identity and upbringing, draws on old insights he has been taught to give an account of a new development." How does his message connect to God's past history with the people? What do these connections tell us about both God and the people?
- "Zechariah shows his awareness of the larger story that is moving forward here. It's a story about a God who keeps showing up to redeem and deliver." How does Jesus both meet and challenge the expectations of salvation in Zechariah's song? How does he both meet and challenge expectations of salvation today?
- How does Zechariah's song reinforce the relationship between Zechariah's son John the Baptist and Jesus?
- "Zechariah describes God's compassion as the impulse behind Jesus's and John's arrivals." Why does this motivation matter? When was a time you and/or your congregation have experienced "the tender mercy of our God" (verse 78)?
- Zechariah's song pictures movement toward "peace" (verse 79), but as Matt notes, "Jesus must go through strife to get there." Why can the way of peace for Christians never be separate from the way to the cross? How are you and your congregation proclaiming and enacting a commitment to the way of peace?

Optional: Play a recording of a musical setting of the Benedictus, or sing together a hymn or song based on the text. Briefly discuss how the music affects what participants hear in and through the text.

THE PROLOGUE TO JOHN'S GOSPEL

Recruit a volunteer to read aloud John 1:1-18, traditionally known as the Prologue to John. Discuss:

- What word or image in John's Prologue most captures your attention or imagination? Why?
- Who is the main actor or "character" in John's Prologue, and what does this actor do?
- Read Genesis 1:1-5. What connections can you make between the Creation story and John's Prologue? How do they help you understand the Prologue's message?
- Read Proverbs 8. What or who is divine Wisdom? What is the relationship between Wisdom and God? between Wisdom and the world? How does John's Prologue reflect "older scripts" about Wisdom from Israel's faith?
- Matt says Israel's Wisdom traditions reminded people that "God's presence and blessing imbue all the ordinary aspects of life and are as close to us as the air we breathe." In what ordinary aspects of your life, if any, have you encountered God?
- What does John's Prologue say about God's Word (Greek *logos*)? How is the claim that God speaks central to Scripture and to both Jewish and Christian faith today?
- What does it mean to identify God's speech with Jesus?
- Matt explains that several ancient philosophers considered the Logos a "grounding principle in the universe...a rational foundation that could provide solid footing for all of humanity's questions about how to live a good or moral life." How is the Prologue's description of the Word like and unlike this philosophical concept?
- How does John's Prologue both identify Jesus with and distinguish Jesus from God? How closely do you identify or distinguish between Jesus and God? Why?
- What does the Prologue's use of father and son imagery (verses 14, 18) tell us about the relationship between God and Jesus? How can this male imagery both reinforce and

challenge social assumptions about being "masculine"?
How easily do you and/or your congregation use masculine
language and imagery for God and Jesus? Why? What role
do other images play in your faith?

- In verse 14, "John doesn't say the Word became *human*,"
  Matt notes, but "*flesh*." What's the difference, and why does
  it matter?

- Matt explains that the verb in verse 14 translated "lived"
  literally means "dwelled in a tent." How does this image
  help you understand the significance of the Word's earthly
  existence?

- What relationship does the Prologue draw between glory,
  grace, and truth (verses 16-17)? How does each of these
  terms help us understand the others in this text?

- Matt says the word translated "heart" in verse 18 is
  better translated "breast," and conveys "intimacy and
  vulnerability." Why are these qualities important in
  understanding God and Jesus's relationship?

- "Jesus later declares that he aims to make the same kind
  of intimacy [with God] possible for the rest of us (John
  17:26)." How much intimacy and vulnerability with God
  do you experience?

CLOSING YOUR SESSION

Read aloud from Matt's book: "The three voices we've lingered
over ... offer us more poetry than precision. ... [They are] full of arresting
images, wordplay, and imagination. ... Advent offers a particularly
appropriate time for us to expand our imagination. ... Maybe we find
ourselves inspired to compose new poems in response."

While reassuring participants (if needed) that you are not asking
them to write full original poems, encourage them to think of a

familiar or original image that communicates something meaningful about God and/or Jesus to them. Invite volunteers to talk briefly about their chosen image; be willing to do so yourself.

Optional: Turn this activity into one using visual images by distributing magazines and newspapers from which participants can choose meaningful pictures.

CLOSING PRAYER

Sing (or read aloud) together at least these verses of "O Come, O Come, Emmanuel" (trans. J. M. Neale, 1851; https://hymnary.org/text/o_come_o_come_emmanuel_and_ransom), an Advent hymn that draws on "old scripts" to express God's new activity in Jesus's coming.

O come, O Key of David, come
and open wide our heavenly home.
Make safe for us the heavenward road
and bar the way to death's abode.
Refrain:
Rejoice! Rejoice! Emmanuel
shall come to you, O Israel.

O come, O Wisdom from on high,
who ordered all things mightily;
to us the path of knowledge show
and teach us in its ways to go. Refrain

O come, O come, Emmanuel,
and ransom captive Israel
that mourns in lonely exile here
until the Son of God appear. Refrain

SESSION 4

THE VOICES OF ANGELS
AND PROPHETS

SESSION GOALS

This session's reading, reflection, discussion, and prayer will help participants:

- Consider Joseph's righteous obedience to God (Matthew 1:18-25) as a model for their own.
- Explore how Matthew interprets the sign of Emmanuel (Isaiah 7:14) as an example of finding continuing significance in stories about God's dependability.
- Examine how the angels' announcement of Jesus's birth to the shepherds (Luke 2:8-14) signals God's intentions for the world.
- Consider Simeon and Anna (Luke 2:25-38) as models of faithful waiting on and witnessing to God.
- Identify signs of God's presence with and commitment to them and humanity that they can offer to others.

BIBLICAL FOUNDATIONS

Now the birth of Jesus the Messiah took place in this way. When his mother Mary had been engaged to Joseph, but before they lived together, she was found to be pregnant from the Holy Spirit. Her husband Joseph, being a righteous man and unwilling to expose her to public disgrace, planned to divorce her quietly. But just when he had resolved to do this, an angel of the Lord appeared to him in a dream and said, "Joseph, son of David, do not be afraid to take Mary as your wife, for the child conceived in her is from the Holy Spirit. She will bear a son, and you are to name him Jesus, for he will save his people from their sins." All this took place to fulfill what had been spoken by the Lord through the prophet:

"Look, the virgin shall become pregnant and give birth to a son,
    and they shall name him Emmanuel,"

which means, "God is with us." When Joseph awoke from sleep, he did as the angel of the Lord commanded him; he took her as his wife but had no marital relations with her until she had given birth to a son, and he named him Jesus.

Matthew 1:18-25

Now in that same region there were shepherds living in the fields, keeping watch over their flock by night. Then an angel of the Lord stood before them, and the glory of the Lord shone around them, and they were terrified. But the angel said to them, "Do not be afraid, for see, I am bringing you good news of great joy for all the people: to you is born this day in the city of David a Savior, who is the Messiah, the Lord. This will be a sign for you: you will find a child wrapped in bands of cloth and lying in a manger." And suddenly there was with the angel a multitude of the heavenly host, praising God and saying,

"Glory to God in the highest heaven,
    and on earth peace among those whom he favors!"

Luke 2:8-14

Guided by the Spirit, Simeon came into the temple, and when the parents brought in the child Jesus to do for him what was customary under the law, Simeon took him in his arms and praised God, saying,

> *"Master, now you are dismissing your servant in peace,*
> > *according to your word,*
> *for my eyes have seen your salvation,*
> > *which you have prepared in the presence of all peoples,*
> *a light for revelation to the gentiles*
> > *and for glory to your people Israel."*

And the child's father and mother were amazed at what was being said about him. Then Simeon blessed them and said to his mother Mary, "This child is destined for the falling and the rising of many in Israel and to be a sign that will be opposed so that the inner thoughts of many will be revealed—and a sword will pierce your own soul, too."

There was also a prophet, Anna the daughter of Phanuel, of the tribe of Asher. She was of a great age, having lived with her husband seven years after her marriage, then as a widow to the age of eighty-four. She never left the temple but worshiped there with fasting and prayer night and day. At that moment she came and began to praise God and to speak about the child to all who were looking for the redemption of Jerusalem.

Luke 2:27-38

BEFORE YOUR SESSION

- Carefully and prayerfully read this session's Biblical Foundations more than once. Note words and phrases that attract your attention and meditate on them. Write down questions you have and try to answer them, consulting trusted Bible commentaries.

- Carefully read chapter 4 of *Voices of Advent* more than once.
- *You will need*: Bibles for in-person participants and/ or screen slides prepared with scripture texts for sharing (identify the translation used); newsprint or a markerboard and markers (for in-person sessions); paper, pens or pencils (in-person).
- If using the DVD or streaming video, preview the session 4 video segment. Choose the best time in your session plan for viewing it.

STARTING YOUR SESSION

Welcome participants. Discuss:

- What does someone who says, "I've had an epiphany!" mean?
- When was a time you "had an epiphany"?
- Matt points out ancient Greek literature included stories called "epiphanies"—"stories about gods becoming manifest to human beings or somehow manifesting their powers in unobvious ways through human affairs." For Christians, the festival of the Epiphany (January 6) celebrates "Jesus's true self becoming manifest or knowable to the whole world." Have you ever "had an epiphany" in this sense, an experience in which God in Jesus Christ was manifest to you? If so, what happened?

Read aloud from Matt's book: "To recognize Christmas as an epiphany, an instance of divine revelation, is important, because it might reorient our perspectives on what it means to encounter God."

As Matt explains, while Jesus's conception is exceptional, Jesus's birth, "as Matthew and Luke narrate it, is mostly unexceptional."

Tell participants that, in this final session together, your group will explore what Matt calls the "tension between extraordinary and ordinary" in these two Christmas stories, asking how it can deepen preparations to celebrate Jesus's birth again.

OPENING PRAYER

Glory to you, O God, in the highest heaven! We praise and adore you for your faithfulness to your creation, for your gracious covenant with your holy people Israel, and for the gift of yourself in your Son, Jesus our Savior. May your Holy Spirit help us hear again the good news of great joy, that we may go with haste and tell it to all who look for redemption and consolation, and even to those who do not: that all your promises find their "Yes" in Christ. Through him, to your glory, we say: **Amen!**

WATCH SESSION VIDEO

Watch the session 4 video segment together. Discuss:

- Which of Matt's statements most interested, intrigued, surprised, or confused you? Why?
- What questions does this video segment raise for you?

JOSEPH: A PORTRAIT OF RIGHTEOUSNESS AND OBEDIENCE

Recruit a volunteer to read aloud Matthew 1:18-25. Discuss:

- How is this story, as Matt says, a story "about God's initiative?"
- What problem do Joseph and Mary face as the story begins?

Why is Joseph thinking about ending his engagement to her?

- Matt explains that Joseph's breaking of his engagement to Mary would involve legal action, possibly the return of her dowry and release from pledges to family members, and "excessive public scrutiny." (Despite common Christian assumptions and anti-Jewish stereotypes, Matthew does not say Mary was facing a death sentence.) How understandable or not do you find his intent to "divorce her quietly" (verse 19), and why?

- Matthew tells us Joseph was "righteous" (verse 19). "Righteous does not mean sanctimonious or too good for everyone else; it means Joseph wants to do the right thing." Who is a righteous person you know or have known, and why? When have you been, tried to be, or wanted to be a righteous person in a difficult situation? What happened?

- How is Joseph's plan to divorce Mary a "threat to the royal lineage of Mary's child" (see 1:16-17, 20)? Why is that lineage an important part of Jesus's identity?

- How does the appearance of an angel in dreams connect this Joseph to the Joseph in the Book of Genesis? Do you think God communicates in and through dreams today? Why or why not? What literal and/or figurative dreams have moved and still move righteous people to "take the story forward as God wills it"?

- Does the angel's message to Joseph solve the problem he and Mary face? Why or why not?

- How does Joseph's experience illuminate the difference between living with obedient trust in God and "facing life with passivity"?

- Matt points out that the angel gives Joseph no *proof*, but only a *promise*, "which is evidently enough for him." Have you or your congregation ever taken action "with limited information" but because you believed God had made a promise? What happened, or is still happening, because you did?

- When, if ever, have you and/or your congregation experienced being obedient to God as "a step-by-step affair"? What do you do to discern "the next best step" when the obedient road is long?

- What makes this story of Jesus's birth both exceptional and unexceptional?

"THEY SHALL NAME HIM EMMANUEL"

Recruit a volunteer to read aloud Isaiah 7:10-16. Before the reading, briefly explain the context: In the eighth century BCE, King Ahaz of Judah (the Southern Kingdom of God's people) is afraid because Israel (the Northern Kingdom of God's people) and Syria are pressuring him to join their alliance against the Assyrian Empire, with whom Ahaz wants to ally. The prophet Isaiah urges Ahaz to trust God instead of military alliances.

After the reading, discuss:

- Why does King Ahaz refuse to answer God's invitation to ask for a sign? Do you believe his stated reason? Why or why not? When, if ever, have you asked or refused to ask God for a sign, and why? What happened?

- What "sign" does Isaiah promise God will give Ahaz? How is it a sign of hope?

- How is the sign to which Isaiah points both exceptional and unexceptional?

- In Hebrew, Isaiah speaks of a "young woman" who is already pregnant. Quoting him from the Septuagint (the 3rd–1st centuries BCE Greek translation of Israel's Scriptures), Matthew speaks of a "virgin" who will become pregnant (1:22-23). How significant do you find these differences, and why? How, if at all, do they shape what you think about the manner and meaning of Jesus's birth?
- What does Matthew mean when he says Jesus's birth "fulfills" Isaiah 7:14? Does the fact that the angel tells Joseph to name Mary's child Jesus, not Emmanuel, undercut Matthew's claim? Why or why not?
- "Christians direct too much animosity on a regular basis toward our Jewish neighbors when, among other things, we insist that biblical passages can have only one correct meaning, and we've figured it out." Do you think acknowledging multiple meanings of the sign of Immanuel/ Emmanuel decreases or increases its significance? Why? Can Christians continue to affirm Jesus as Emmanuel without continuing or encouraging anti-Jewish attitudes? Why or why not?
- "Matthew reminds us that stories—especially stories about God's dependability—can be true more than once and true in more than one way." What stories about God's dependability—from Scripture, from your faith tradition, from your congregation, from your family—have you found to be true more than once and in more than one way, and how?
- "We don't see it yet in this passage from Matthew, but there's a sense of pending danger implied by referring to another baby as Emmanuel." How does the story of King Herod's response to Jesus's birth (Matthew 2) "illustrate how dangerous Christmas is," as Matt says? Why does

the promise of God-with-us threaten those who wield
and cherish worldly power? How does the promise spark
resistance *from* and *to* "tyrants of this world" today?

- Matt says the woman who would name "a child born into
  dangerous circumstances" Emmanuel "knew something
  about the brazenness of hope." How so? When, if ever,
  have you expressed a "brazen" hope in God? How and
  why? What happened?

THE ANGELS' MESSAGE TO SHEPHERDS ABOUT THE MESSIAH

Recruit volunteers to read aloud Luke 2:1-14, reading as the
narrator and the angel of the Lord, with all participants reading aloud
together as the heavenly host in verse 14. Discuss:

- Matt notes no historical evidence outside Luke confirms
  the imperial census (verses 1-3); rather, Luke is "calling
  attention to the Roman Empire's extensive power over
  people, their movements, and their futures. But not
  their hopes." When and where do you see governments
  (your own or others) exercising or attempting to exercise
  imperial-like power over people? How do you respond?
- "The Bible on the whole provides very little information
  about angels," says Matt. What, if anything, do you believe
  about angels, and why? Do you believe you have ever
  encountered angels? Why or why not?
- The "angel of the Lord" says to the shepherds, as biblical
  angels often say, "Do not be afraid" (verse 10; other
  examples include Daniel 10:12; Matthew 28:5; Mark 16:6;
  Luke 1:13, 30; Acts 27:24). Why is "Fear not!" such a
  common angelic greeting?

- The angel says he brings "good news" (verse 10), or "gospel," which Matt notes was a word widely used in the ancient Roman world, including for imperial proclamations or propaganda. How do you tend to react when people say they have "good news" for you, and why? What makes news "good" in your estimation?

- What makes the angel's news "remarkable," as Matt calls it? What is the unremarkable "sign" (verse 12) that will confirm this news for the shepherds? When was a time an unremarkable sight held remarkable significance for you, and why?

- Matt points out Luke's reference to "the heavenly host" (verse 13) is a reference to an angelic army. How is this army like and unlike an earthly army? Why does God use this army to herald Jesus's birth?

- Much Roman propaganda, Matt notes, "boasted about the peace Rome brought" and called Augustus, the first emperor, "savior." What "hint of protest," if any, do you hear against imperial power in the angels' message? What does their message suggest about disruptive or dangerous aspects of Christmas?

- The title "Messiah" (verse 11; Greek, "Christ") means "Anointed One," someone "appointed and commissioned for a special purpose," as prophets, priests, and kings sometimes are in the Old Testament. As Matt explains, not all first-century Jewish people expected a Messiah, and no single messianic "job description" existed; however, among those who looked for the Messiah, expectations often included God raising up a deliverer; a new age of righteousness, peace, and security; and resurrection of the dead. Why did Jesus's followers come to use this title for

him? How meaningful a title do you find it for him,
and why?

- "The Gospels, particularly Matthew and Luke, lift up the
  importance of the Messiah's connection to King David,"
  the shepherd boy from Bethlehem who was anointed king
  (1 Samuel 16:11-13) and came to be remembered as Israel's
  greatest monarch. What expectations and hopes might
  Jesus's birth "in the city of David" raise (verse 11)?

- What responsibilities and traits of shepherds make them
  appropriate images of and metaphors for faithful rulers in
  Scripture (examples: Jeremiah 23:1-4; Ezekiel 34:23-24;
  Micah 5:2-5a)? What other images might convey the same
  meaning today?

- So far from being "ancient society's worst people," as often
  claimed or implied, shepherds were ordinary, powerless
  people. What makes these shepherds near Bethlehem an
  especially appropriate audience for the announcement of
  Jesus's birth?

TWO PROPHETS IN THE TEMPLE

Recruit three volunteers to read aloud Luke 2:(22-26), 27-38: the
narrator, Simeon, and Anna (verses 36-38, though Luke gives her no
direct dialogue). Discuss:

- What does Luke's record of Joseph and Mary's trip to
  Jerusalem with the infant Jesus show us about their
  relationship to Jewish law and tradition (verses 22-24; see
  Leviticus 12)?

- How are Simeon and Anna both ordinary and extraordinary
  individuals? How do both of them model faithful, active
  waiting on God? What "wise, experienced people" you
  know or have known do they remind you of, and why?

- Luke says the Holy Spirit guides Simeon to the Temple. Do you believe the Spirit has ever led you to be in a particular place for a particular reason? If so, when, and what happened?
- How does Simeon's praise of God (verses 29-32) reflect God's faithfulness to him, personally? to God's people Israel? to the world? (Consider also Genesis 12:1-3; 18:18; Isaiah 42:6-7; 60:1-3.)
- "The thrust of Simeon's claim" about what God is doing in Jesus "is all about expansion, inclusion, and belonging." When and how have you seen Jesus's community live out an expansively inclusive vision of who belongs? When and how have you seen it fail to do so? How, specifically, does your congregation live in expansive and inclusive ways?
- How will Jesus be "a sign that will be opposed" (verse 34)? When and how, if at all, do you see Jesus sparking opposition today? What, if anything, do you do in response?
- To what do you think Simeon refers when he says "a sword will pierce" Mary's soul (verse 35)? How is what Simeon anticipates true for anyone who loves and cares for a child, and how will it be unique for Mary?
- Why does Anna praise God? How does Isaiah 52:8-10 help us better understand and appreciate her praise, as Luke summarizes it?
- How is Anna a model for speaking to others about Jesus?

CLOSING YOUR SESSION

Read aloud from Matt's book: "When preachers deliver sermons [about God's reliability and ultimate intentions] on Christmas Eve, I imagine many in the congregation are saying in their heads, 'Ha!

Prove it.' These promises don't lend themselves to easy proof.... The preacher—or you or I—can offer only assorted signs of God's commitment to humanity and to the skeptic in the pew. Those signs of God's presence may look rather low-key and ordinary.... [But t]hey are signs that become more vivid to those who are curious and who are willing to take the next step in trust."

Invite participants to identify specific signs—even and especially "low-key and ordinary" ones—of God's presence with and commitment to them and humanity that they would offer to "the skeptic in the pew," or remind themselves of when *they* are that skeptic.

Thank participants for having shared this study of *Voices of Advent* with you. Ask participants what the most memorable or important thing they have learned from the study is, and/or one big question they still have. If you have not already, make plans for your next study together.

CLOSING PRAYER

Sing (or read aloud) together "Hark! The Herald Angels Sing" (Charles Wesley, 1734; https://hymnary.org/text/hark_the_herald _angels_sing_glory_to) to remember Isaiah and Matthew's proclamations of Emmanuel, the angels' announcement of Jesus's birth, and God's call to us to live as Christ's heralds:

Hark! the herald angels sing,
"Glory to the newborn King:
peace on earth, and mercy mild,
God and sinners reconciled!"
Joyful, all ye nations, rise,
join the triumph of the skies;
with th'angelic hosts proclaim,

"Christ is born in Bethlehem!"
Refrain:
Hark! the herald angels sing,
"Glory to the newborn King"

Christ, by highest heaven adored,
Christ, the everlasting Lord,
late in time behold him come,
offspring of the Virgin's womb:
veiled in flesh the Godhead see;
hail th'incarnate Deity,
pleased with us in flesh to dwell,
Jesus, our Immanuel. Refrain

Hail the heaven-born Prince of Peace!
Hail the Sun of Righteousness!
Light and life to all he brings,
risen with healing in his wings.
Mild he lays his glory by,
born that we no more may die,
born to raise us from the earth,
born to give us second birth. Refrain

www.ingramcontent.com/pod-product-compliance
Lightning Source LLC
LaVergne TN
LVHW031248021125
824796LV00007B/17